To Matan, Micah
& Madison

Adventure is out there!

Love,
Marilyn & 2/16/21

Special thanks to everyone ever, but especially to my Opinionation Station who were always so wonderful in lending thoughts, ideas and opinions. Love to Mae for the photos, my amazing friends for their editing help, the boy who always believed, 'Mani, Marry and Momo, Colby's "Freek Familee", and most of all to Momsie, Daddy, Punkie and Lene, who may have questioned my crazy imagination, but always ran with it.

And to Ellie—who never questioned anything. I love you most of ever.
"Look at all the magic!" ❤

For anyone who's ever had a Colby of their own.

Maribeth McCarthy has always loved to tell stories. This is mostly because she comes from a big Irish family, and telling stories is just what they do. She also loves teddy bears, singing, snowflakes, theatre, Christmas, waterfalls, being a twin, and making people happy. And of course, she loves you— because you are awesome. She has written plays and books and gone on many exciting adventures.

But that's another story. :)

Written and Illustrated by Maribeth McCarthy
Imagery clean up and book layout design by Shannon McCarthy

Printed in the United States of America
First Printing, 2018
ISBN-13: 978-1718657199
ISBN-10: 1718657196

Colby and the First Day Ever

Written and Illustrated by Maribeth McCarthy

Sometimes people ask about where you come from.

Like, are you from a big place or small place?

Were there a lot of buildings?

Were there animals?

Were there others like you?

I do not know where I came from.
All I remember is being asleep...
and then I woke up.

I was snuggled into something very warm;
I think it was a very fluffy blankee. I was quite sleepy.

I yawned, and when I did my left eye opened and
there was a very pretty lady standing in front of me.
She had bright red hair and big blue eyes.

She smiled a very big smile at me and whispered, "Hello."

"Hellooo," I said back to her, still yawning a bit.

"Who are you?"

"I'm here to take you home," she smiled, holding me close.

"Home?" I asked her.

"Home." She kissed me on the top of my head. It felt nice. I liked her right away. "Are you ready, Colby?" she asked.

"Colby?" I didn't know who she meant.

"Colby." She giggled, just a little.

"That's what I've decided to call you."

"Cooooooolbeee" I moved the word around in my mouth.

"Col beeeee. COL-be! Colby!" I giggled, same as her.

"I like that name! Is it really mine?"

"Yes, it is," she smiled, taking my hand and walking
with me down a very long hallway.

"Is it a good name?" I asked her.
"Yes, yes it is a very good name." She just kept smiling!

"What is your name?" I wondered if it was Colby too, since
  it was such a very good name.

"Well, I was hoping maybe...if it's okay with you...
  I could be your Mommy."

"My Maay?" I tried to make the word right, like I did with mine.
"My-ee?" I tried again and even though it was not the same as
  the way she said it, I think she knew what I meant.

"Yes." She settled me into a seat and buckled me in tight. "Do you know what a Mommy is?"

I did! I knew what a Mommy was even though I had never had one. I remember dreaming about one while I was asleep.

"A Maay is someone who wants to take care of you. A Maay will kiss you and make you feel better if you are sick and she will look after you always, no matter what."

"Exactly." She kissed my head again. "A Mommy is someone who loves you more than anything else."

"She loves you most of **EVER?**" I asked, my eyes wide.

She giggled again, "Yes."

"Loves you..." I whispered to myself. I did not know what that word meant. I was just about to ask her when she said–

"Are you ready to go home, Colby?"

I looked around at the seat that held me tight and the lady who wanted to bring me home–the lady who named me and said she wanted to take care of me. I never felt anything like it before. It made me happy, so I looked up at her and said, "I am ready!–Maay."

Maay drove us to a big house, bigger than anything I had ever seen before. She opened the door, helped me out, and carried me inside. "I hope you like your new home, Colby," she said as she closed the door behind us.

Well, I already liked her and my new name so I was pretty sure I would like this home place, too. Especially if we got to be together. As we walked on, we passed a big mirror.

"Whoa!" I looked closer. "Who are they, Maay?"

Maay pointed to them. "That's you and me, kiddo. **That's us. We're a family now."**

I looked closer. I was little, littler than Maay. I had soft brown fur and big brown eyes. Maay had very bright red hair and no fur. Her cheek was soft and smooth when I touched it. Mine was soft and furry. I had big ears and Maay had little ones. **We did not look anything alike. That made me sad and I felt something wet come from my eye.**

"Colby, honey, what's wrong?"
Maay caught the wet thing
with her hand.

"I just..." I breathed in
through hiccups.
"You said we were a
family but I do not
look anything like you.
So how can we be family?"

"Oh..." She gently hugged
me closer. "You don't have
to worry about that. Not at all."

"But–" I hiccuped. "But I–"

"Shhhhh..." She held me up higher and I looked
 in the mirror again. "What do you see?"

"I see us. But we are different. You have blue eyes.
 And I have brown–"

"Eyes. Yup. We both have eyes."

"And your ears are little and mine–"

"Hear things just the same as mine do."
 She tickled me behind my ear and I giggled.
 She giggled, too.

"And we both smile— see?" She pointed at us in the mirror, smiling very big. **She was right!**

"And laugh!" She tickled me a little, and we DID both laugh! "And look, I have a nose and you have a nose. Boop!" She pushed on my tiny nose. I giggled again.

"Boop!" I did it back to her nose, which was bigger than mine. She laughed, too. "But what about the other things? The things that are different?"

"Well," she said thoughtfully, "That's really nothing at all. Being different is what makes us special. It makes us like no one else in the whole world. Isn't that an incredible thing? To be one of something? There will only ever be one Colby— one you. Just one. In all the world."

"In all the world…" I smiled a little. **The world was a very big place. I suddenly felt very important to be in it.** And sleepy. I yawned. I guess it must be very tiring being the only one of you in the whole world.

Maay saw me yawning. "I think it's time for a little sleep. It's been a very big day, hasn't it?"

"It has..." I started, before drifting off to sleep in her arms. Maay walked me down the hall into a room with a tiny bed, just for me.

"Goodnight, Colby," she soothed, tucking me into the very fluffy blankets. "I love you."

"I lo–" My eyes opened wide and I remembered what I wanted to ask Maay before. "Maay? What is love?"

"Oh..." She looked at me, smiling. "That is a very big question, and you are very sleepy. But for now, I'll just say...love is caring about someone else. Love is wanting someone else to be happy– for all their dreams to come true."

"Is that why you love me, Maay?
Did I make a dream come true?"

"Yes, you did." Maay's eyes got a little shiny.
"I waited a long time for you."

That made me feel very special. In all the world, Maay had
been waiting for ME! I smiled again and it turned into a yawn.
"Tell me more about love, Maay? Please?"

"Well...I think a good way to put it is that it's like you've been
asleep for a very long time, and you're finally waking up."
I heard her whisper as I drifted off to sleep.

"Goodnight, my Colby". She touched my nose softly again.
"**I love you.**"

"Goodnight, Maay..." I wrapped the soft blanket tighter around me.
"**I love you, too...**"

While I was asleep I dreamed of all sorts of things. I dreamed of Maay and me going on adventures, and baking cookies, and planting a garden, and her taking care of me, and me taking care of her, too.

I dreamed of friends I would find and other people who would become family like Maay. I dreamed of the day I came alive. It was not the same way other people come alive but I think that is okay. I also do not look much like anyone else...but I think that is okay, too. **Because now I am here, and we are a family, and I am loved.**

I felt something warm on my face. I yawned
very loudly and my eyes slowly opened to a very
bright day. There was Maay, waiting for me!
And I felt something inside me, all light and fluffy.
I think it was love! When I looked at Maay again,
after rubbing the sleepies from my eyes, I was
sure of it. And Maay was right! It felt JUST the
way she said!

I was asleep for a very long time...

And now I am awake.

Made in the USA
Lexington, KY
07 June 2018